TEENS WITH PHYSICAL DISABILITIES

Real-life Stories of Meeting the Challenges

Glenn Alan Cheney

—Issues in Focus—

ENSLOW PUBLISHERS, INC.

44 Fadem Road	P.O. Box 38
Box 699	Aldershot
Springfield, N.J. 07081	Hants GU12 6BP
U.S.A.	U.K.

For Kitty

Copyright © 1995 by Glenn Alan Cheney

All rights reserved.

No part of this book may be reproduced by any means
without the written permission of the publisher.

Library of Congress Cataloging-in-Publication Data

Cheney, Glenn Alan.
    Teens with physical disabilities: real-life stories of meeting the challenges / Glenn Alan
Cheney.
       p. cm. — (Issues in focus)
    Includes bibliographical references and index.
    ISBN 0-89490-625-9
    1. Physically handicapped teenagers—United States—Attitudes—Juvenile literature.
[1. Physically handicapped. 2. Youth—Attitudes.] I. Title. II Series: Issues in focus
(Springfield, N.J.)
HV888.5.C456 1995
362.4'04'0835—dc20   94-3603
                                        CIP
                                          AC

Printed in the United States of America

10 9 8 7 6 5 4 3 2

Illustration Credits: Glenn Alan Cheney, pp. 8, 18, 28, 50, 80, 92; Anne Forbis,
p. 62; Eric Slomanson, p. 38.

Cover Illustration: Dale Wittner, PhotoSeattle

Contents

Introduction

This is not a book about physical disabilities. It is about how a handful of young people are coping with physical disabilities.

Before we say another word, let's make sure we understand that key word, *disability*, and its counterpart, *handicap*. A person *has* a disability. In the case of physical disabilities, it's the legs or hands that don't work, the eyes that can't see, the ears that don't hear. A handicap is a limitation or barrier. Limitations can be in the inability to walk up stairs, pick things up, see a face, hear a voice, and so on. It is the difficulty the person has in dealing with some aspects of his or her environment. Even though there isn't much that can be done about many disabilities, limitations can be overcome. The wheelchair helps overcome the inability to walk. But then the limitation comes to life again when the chair reaches a barrier such as the bottom of a stairway. A barrier can be as simple as a street curb or as complex as an attitude.

As long as we're dealing with terms, let's make it clear that a *person with a disability* is not a *disabled person*. If you can understand the difference between those terms, you can understand the extra problem these people face. It isn't just their disabilities. It's the fact that they are people first. It's the way others perceive them. It's a barrier called prejudice.

This book presents the thoughts and experiences of a few teenagers with physical disabilities. It does not approach the vast area of mental disabilities, nor does it touch on the complete range of physical disabilities and chronic illnesses, which include asthma, diabetes, bone disorders, nervous disorders, obesity, emphysema, heart disease, amputation, cancer, contagious diseases, traumatic brain injury, and many genetic abnormalities.

Sadly, the list of mental and physical disabilities is far longer than any one book can cover. But, again, this is not a book about disabilities. It's about eight people. One was born deaf, another was born with rheumatoid arthritis. One gradually developed the worsening symptoms of muscular dystrophy. One developed blindness at the age when other kids are just getting good at baseball. One was born with cerebral palsy. Three others became paralyzed in their mid-teens, the years when young people normally start gaining the independence of adulthood.

Like every other teenager in the world, these kids have had to grapple with all the radical changes brought on by adolescence. They've had to develop their individual personalities while at the same time fitting in with their peers. They've had to decide what was right and wrong and what to do about the temptations they've found at the threshold of adulthood. They've had to deal with bodies that were becoming quite different from the ones they had as young children.

On top of all that, they've had to deal with a disability that has limited their activities and set them apart from the crowd. Maybe they've missed classes because an elevator wasn't working. Or they've missed a party because they couldn't drive there or, worse, weren't invited. Or maybe their clothes don't fit right because their bodies are different. Or people are uncomfortable talking with them because they confuse a physical problem with a personality problem. It's a lot for a teenager to put up with.

Though the people in this book have very different disabilities, they share a single desire: to fit in with their peers. Like virtually every other person with a disability, they wish they could be appreciated for who they are and what they can do. Their physical imperfections are insignificant compared to their abilities and the person inside the body.

Adapting to a disability is a lot like growing up. It's a process of moving from blissful certainties, like those of childhood, into an adult's recognition of how life can be painful and hard. Like the process of maturing, it's a movement from ignorance to awareness. Individuals have to learn to control their world in new ways. They learn to plan, figuring ahead how they'll get up stairs or find the right door or communicate with someone. They face the mountainous obstacle of emotional depression. They figure out what they have to do and how they have to approach life. In short, they adapt.

Compensating for a physical disability is only half the battle. Learning to use sign language, read Braille, or lift oneself out of a wheelchair and into a car doesn't erase the effects of a disability. The person as a whole must change. This change may involve accepting the reality of a new disability or readjusting one's goals and aspirations in life or simply appreciating everyday events, such as going outside in the fresh air, that people without disabilities often take for granted. Ironically, sometimes a negative change in body can bring about a positive change in a person.

But it's not an easy growth. Society doesn't always offer much help. In uncountable thousands of ways, society helps everyone learn how to mature and how to face the world. Open any book, watch any film, listen in on any conversation, and you'll get a glimpse of how someone *without a disability* is handling life. But how often does a person with a disability get to share the feelings and experience of someone in the same predicament? For that matter, how often does the perfectly healthy individual get to share that experience? Opportunities are few. This book is meant to be one.

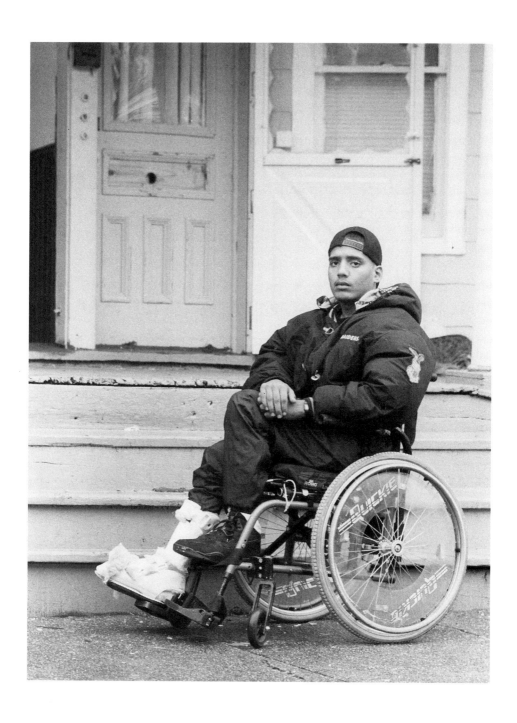

1

Donny Dumeng

Donny Dumeng is eighteen and lives in a rough neighborhood in the Connecticut city with the highest per capita murder rate in the state. His parents are from Puerto Rico but don't live together. He lives with his mother, who cleans offices at a tea company, and his little sister and her new baby. He's a big fan of pepperoni pizza and rap music. It's all he wants to hear. He's not sure what kind of career he'd like to pursue, but he's thinking about computers. Not a bad field, if he can finish high school. He dropped out of the ninth grade when somebody shot a bullet into his spine.

"I was going to the store, right? And I saw this friend of mine, and I started talking to him. Then these two black dudes walked by and started shooting at two other Puerto Ricans. It was over some drug thing, but since I was there, I was one of the ones that got shot. I fell down. I thought I was dreaming, but I wasn't. I was trying to get back up, but I couldn't feel my legs. I thought I got shot there. I kept saying to my friend, 'What happen my legs? What happen my legs?'

"My brother drove me to the hospital. I was awake the whole time and kept telling him to tell my mother I just got shot in the legs, that's all, so she wouldn't faint or anything. Then they X-rayed me and found out I had a bullet in my spine—a '.380.' It was in a spot where they couldn't take it out, and it's still in there. I was in critical condition and had to stay in that hospital for two months, lying flat on my back the whole time. I couldn't move anything from my chest on down. I started getting bedsores so they took me to Newington Children's Hospital. I had to stay two more months. The whole time I just kept saying, 'I want to go home, I want to go home.' I gave the nurses a hard time, cussing them, throwing stuff, and not doing my care exercises. I was just worrying about my mother. I didn't let them teach me anything about my condition or how to deal with it, so they finally just sent me home.

"I couldn't handle it. I missed all the fun I used to have, like riding a dirt bike. I just wanted to die. I didn't care about anything. I started doing all kinds of drugs and then dope. A *lot* of dope. I mean *heroin.* That stuff's bad. Once you start, you can't just kick it. So for a year I just be hanging out and doing dope, doing dope, doing dope. I don't know how my mother never found out. She kept asking me what I did with all my money. I got skinnier and skinnier and was staying out late all the time, not going to school and not taking any care of myself. Finally my mother told me she knew what I was doing. I can't lie to my mother, so I told her yes, it was true. She tried to get me into programs, but I kept running away.

"For a while I got around in a wheelchair, but then I bought me a car. A guy from Puerto Rico who got shot and can't walk took me down to a big parking lot near the beach and showed me how to drive without your legs. You use a stick to push on the brake and the gas. It wasn't legal. I just did it.

"After that, I be sitting in the car all the time. I had crackheads running around delivering dope for me. That's how I got money for my own habit. Nobody messed with me because I already had a reputation for being bad. Before my accident I already shot a few people. I shot my aunt for smacking me. I shot my cousin because of a girl. I shot a black dude who was slapping my sister. I shot another black dude who I was trying to rob. He turned around and started running, and I shot him in the back. I think that's why I got shot in the back. All that was before my accident. I was real hyper. I sniffed coke and smoked weed, and then any little thing would set me off and I be yelling at everybody, beating on my sisters for no reason, all kinds of stuff. I was hyper, man. I was crazy and bad. I wouldn't let my sisters see nobody. That was back when I could walk, but after the accident, while I was in the hospital, I couldn't protect them, so my two little sisters both got pregnant.

"About a year after the accident, I got sick again. Real bad pressure sores from sitting in the car all the time. I was close to dying. I went to a hospital near home, but my friends started bringing me weed. They used to push me outside so we could get high. I was in that hospital for a month, and I was still bad, cussing at the nurses and everything. They finally made me go home. Visiting nurses would come see me, but some of them would refuse to do anything with me because the sores were so bad, all infected and everything. The nurses said they were going to turn us in to the state department of child welfare if I didn't go to a hospital. My mother kept begging me to go to Newington Children's Hospital again, but I didn't want to go because it was too far from home. But then my sister had a baby and we were afraid he'd catch my infections, so I agreed to go if she promised to visit me every week.

"I sniffed a *lot* of dope the day I went. I was real high. But I went clean as soon as I got there. This time the hospital really saved me. I was there for a whole year 'cause I had to have operations and then recuperate. A lot of my friends were coming to visit me. Some of them had been shot and were in wheelchairs. They told me, 'You got to handle it, man. You got to deal with it. Don't let it stay in your mind. Learn to keep on doing what you used to do back when you could walk.'

"One thing I did right this time was to learn what they were trying to teach me at the hospital. Before I left I knew how to take care of myself in the world. I learned how to transfer by myself, which means to move from the wheelchair to a car or a chair without help. I learned how to get dressed by myself. Before I learned that I had to have my sisters or a home aide help me. I learned all kinds of stuff. That was a good hospital, I got to say that. They saved me.

"One of the nurses, she kind of liked me. Now she's my lady and she comes down to visit me. She's real fine. There's still a lot of stuff I can do. But I'm not getting married or anything right now. I'm too young for that.

"I'm not hyper the way I used to be. I keep calm. I stay at home. I don't go messing around the streets and staying out late. It's bad out there, worse than it used to be. I know a *lot* of guys who got shot. Some of them died. Some of them ended up in wheelchairs. Some of them went to jail. I know this one crackhead who's out on the street in a wheelchair begging money, always asking for a dollar or whatever. If I got a dollar I give it to him and tell him to go home, get off the street. He didn't get shot. I don't know what it was that made him not be able to walk. I think it was shooting dope. Something like that. He got sick or something.

"People give me money, too. Drug dealers. I don't ask for it. They just give it to me. They feel sorry for me 'cause they know I used to walk. And 'cause they respect me. They know how bad I used to be. So sometimes they give me money, and nobody messes with me, except sometimes somebody takes advantage of me. Like I'll give somebody some money to go get me a pack of cigarettes and they won't come back. I hate that.

"Sometimes my family puts on a attitude. I ask for some help or something and they say, 'Go on and do it your ownself.' Like as if I could have got up and done it. Sometimes they say I like being this way 'cause I don't have to do nothin' and I get a check for $434 every month. They be crazy. I don't want a check. I want my legs back. Who wants to wait for a check in a wheelchair?

"One thing I do now that I didn't used to is play basketball. I never used to do any kind of sports, but now I do it just to get out and do something. I'm on a team called the Park City Rollers. We play teams from all over the place—Rhode Island, Boston. We're pretty good. It's more fun than staying home watching TV and making myself miserable like the way I was before. I used to be real miserable.

"I'm trying to get my own apartment in a special project for people with handicaps. I know a lot of people over there. It's all set up inside for a wheelchair. I can do everything to take care of myself except cook, but I'll just send out for pizza every day. That's good enough for me.

"As soon as I get my apartment, I'm going to start doing something with my life. I want to go back to school, and then I'll think about what kind of a career I want. I was thinking about computers, but I don't know. Maybe I'll get a job in the post office, in back, where they sort out the mail.

"If I hear about another kid who gets shot and has to be in a wheelchair, I'm going to tell him he's got to deal with it. You can't let it stay in your mind all the time. You can't go feeling sorry for yourself 'cause nobody's going to feel sorry for you and help you do everything. The only one that's going to do that is your mother. You have to get out and start doing the things you always did. You have to learn how to do it. You can always do a lot of stuff if you learn how.

"If I hear about kids messing around like I used to, I tell 'em they better stay off the street and stay off drugs. When they ask me why, I tell them it's because everything comes back at you. You act crazy and something crazy's going to happen to you. You bother people, you're going to be bothered. You run around with a gun, you're going to get shot. If anybody wants to know how you know, you tell them Donny told you."

Questions about Gunshot Wounds

How does getting shot cause paralysis?

A bullet of any caliber can cause permanent or temporary damage to the spine, neck, or brain. The brain controls the arms, the legs, and other parts of the body by transmitting and receiving "messages" called neurons, which travel through the spinal cord. If the pathway of those neurons is broken, part of the body cannot respond to "messages" from the brain. Often the brain cannot receive sensations from a part of the body. Depending on where the spinal or brain damage occurs, the paralysis can be partial or virtually total.

Is there any cure for paralysis due to a gunshot wound?

It depends on the wound. Damage to brain cells is permanent, but sometimes, with therapy, the brain can find a way to work around the injured area and regain control of some body movement. Damage to the spinal cord is permanent, with very little recovery of related movement. Generally, the higher the damage is in the spine, the higher the area of paralysis in the body.

How can I keep from getting shot?

In violent neighborhoods, there is no perfect protection from gunfire. Though you're safer indoors than out (unless there's a gun in the house), bullets from high-powered guns can go through walls of brick or wood and can travel over a mile. The best protection is to avoid situations that might attract gunfire. Drug dealing is the most common source of bystanders being shot. Accidents with guns in the home are the most common cause of gunshot wounds. Robberies are a less common cause, but shootings do occur there also.

The best protective measures, then, are obvious:

1. Avoid people involved in dealing drugs and areas where this activity takes place.

2. Either don't keep a gun at home, or keep an unloaded gun locked up, well hidden, out of the reach of children, and separate from ammunition.

3. In the case of robbery, stay calm, do not resist, and hand over valuables.

4. Report illegal handguns to the police.

Will a bulletproof vest keep me safe?

Bulletproof vests do not stop all bullets and do not protect all the vital parts of the body. A bullet that hits up against the spine without penetrating the vest can do enough damage to cause paralysis or even death.

2

Lisa Morgan

Lisa's so quick with a giggle you'd think she'd been your best friend for years. Like every other kid in the world, she likes tacos, ice cream, brownies, chocolate, and just about anything else that's not especially good for you. Given some free time after school, she's as likely as any eighteen-year-old to go hang out at the mall, or take a walk on the beach. She gets around quite well, thanks to a nice new set of hips and knees. She still has juvenile rheumatoid arthritis (JRA), and though less severe cases may go into remission, Lisa's probably won't. But that's not going to stop her. When Lisa wants something, she goes for it, and between her giggle and great determination, she gets it.

"When I was five years old, a doctor said I'd probably never walk. Since a few months after I was born, juvenile rheumatoid arthritis has been eating at the stuff that protects my joints from the bones that work inside them. Dead tissue builds up, and the joints get all inflamed and don't develop right. So I've been in constant pain since I was eight months old—but in a way, it's good it started that early. To me, the pain is normal, so I don't notice it.

"The real pain is in what I can't do. I have curves in my spine, so I can't bend over and pick something up. My left elbow is locked, so I can't comb my hair and blow-dry it at the same time. My feet are turned inward, so I can't walk very far. I couldn't walk at all, except with crutches or a walker, until I had my old hips and knees taken out and replaced with artificial ones. I felt pain then. I had to go through six operations and stay in traction for eight weeks. I had to take morphine for pain and administer it myself every seven minutes. It's all I thought about. I wouldn't talk to anybody, and I kept the shade drawn in my room so no sunlight could come in. My mother kept saying, 'Don't watch the clock,' but I couldn't help it. When they finally took me off morphine, I shook and shook and got so hyper. I just wanted to get OUT of there. I listened to Michael Bolton sing 'When I'm Back on My Feet Again,' over and over, identifying with every word of it.

"When I got out of the hospital, my parents gave me something I always wanted: a cat. She's beautiful, all white and fluffy with long hair. But she's too much like me. She does what she wants to do, no matter what. If I want to hold her in my lap, since I can't bend over, I have to tempt her onto a chair with some food or something. It's pretty frustrating, but I love her that way.

"After I got these new hips and knees, I could walk. That was about two years ago, when I was seventeen. Until then, I couldn't go out on my own, couldn't even get up stairs without crawling. Now I can drive. My father rigged the ignition so I can reach it, which normally I couldn't because my arms are short. He also put a board behind the seat to move me up closer to the steering wheel. He even built this pulley thing so I could get my crutches up off the back seat floor. They kept falling out, though. It's just as easy to leave them on the seat.

"Anyway, now when I want to go somewhere, I go. Nothing stops me.

"I have a friend, Melissa, who has JRA, but hers is different from mine, a lot less severe. Hers comes and goes, and to look at her, you wouldn't know she has it. Every once in a while, it flares up. Her temperature can get so high she hallucinates. She'll be in terrible pain for a while, but then it goes away. Since she looks perfectly healthy most of the time, sometimes people don't sympathize with her so much when she says her joints ache.

"At graduation, in high school, I was afraid the stage was going to stop me. More than anything in the world I wanted to walk up those stairs to get my diploma. And I did it. Everybody was clapping and cheering, and I made it. It was the best moment of my life. And I got not only my diploma but also ten awards.

"This wasn't at the regular public school, which wasn't accessible, but at a public technical school. It was really a great experience. I liked it a lot. We had to pick a trade and study for it. I picked graphic arts, which I don't really love, but it was okay. I got to run the printing press even though they said I couldn't manage it. They wanted me to just stay with the computer, which not even the teachers knew how to work and which meant I'd be cut off from everybody else. They said I wanted to run the press just because I wanted to go socialize with the other kids, which might have been true, but even so, how come other kids could do it and I couldn't? I *hate* it when people tell me I can't do something. I know what I can do and can't do. When they finally let me run the press, what do you know, given a little help, I could do it. Surprise, surprise.

"The school had an elevator, and that was the only way I could get upstairs or back down. But it was a rickety old thing that was broken half the time, so I had to miss class. My mother kept calling them, but it kept

22

happening. Since the school couldn't legally carry me up and down the stairs, I'd have to stay in a room downstairs and do my work. This wasn't so bad, though, because the teachers there were great.

"No real relationships developed from school, but I did have two boyfriends. One didn't last too long, but the other was pretty serious. I had dates to my junior and senior proms and got out there on the dance floor on my crutches and danced. One guy was a foot and a half taller than me, so he just picked me up and we danced that way. Everybody thought that was great. They wanted me to do it again so they could take a picture for the yearbook, but I said no way. It's kind of a neat way to dance, but embarrassing.

"The whole time my feet were killing me because of my shoes. It's impossible to find dress shoes when your feet are like mine. The closest size was way too small. I could have worn my sneakers, but who wants to wear high tops to a prom?

"The problem with finding a boyfriend is finding one who's mature enough and who doesn't have to rely on other people. I don't like guys who act like jerks, and I don't like going to crazy parties where everybody acts stupid. I don't know what's going to happen when I start college in the fall. I want to study, but everybody says I'm just going to have fun.

"I want to get married someday and have a family. I can't have a baby, though. I mean, I could get pregnant, but because of the curves in my spine, I'd have to stay lying on my back the whole nine months. And then there'd be a chance the baby would have JRA because it's genetic. There's no way I would let that happen. Like, it's okay if it happened to me. I can live with it. I'd rather it happened to me than to anyone I know. I mean, it made me the person I am and I'm happy with who I am, and if I could go back and not have the disease in the first place but then not be who I am, I wouldn't do it.

"But at the same time, I wouldn't want to cause somebody else to have these problems. I've been in and out of hospitals all my life. I saw a picture of me when I was just a baby. I had a huge bruise on my forehead because that was the only place left where they could put an IV. When I was older, a doctor said he could scrape the dead tissue from out of my joints and I'd feel better. I have a picture of me after the operation in traction on Halloween, all made up like a clown and I couldn't even get out of bed. It was a waste of an operation because I still had JRA and more dead tissue started building up the next day.

"I'd like to adopt a baby, but with all the stories I've been hearing, it scares me. I couldn't pick the kid up off the floor, let alone all the toys and stuff. I can change diapers, but I can't take something out of the oven. I could tie the kid's shoes, but I'll never be able to tie my own. And anyway, adopting a baby is good, but I'll never be able to look down and see my own face in somebody else.

"Sometimes I wonder what I'd tell a kid—my own or somebody else's—if she had JRA. I think I'd tell her not to let it stop her. I'd tell her to live life as normally as you can and don't believe them when they tell you can't do something. Be yourself. Do what you can do, and don't let anybody tell you what you can't."

Questions about Juvenile Rheumatoid Arthritis

How serious is juvenile rheumatoid arthritis (JRA)?

About 165,000 children and young adults in the United States have arthritis, and 70,000 of them have JRA. The most common symptom in the four types of JRA is inflammation of a joint or several joints. The swelling can cause severe pain and stiffness. Naturally, a person with arthritis will tend not to use joints that hurt. The inactivity can cause problems in muscles, which then cause deformity in the joint. Also, joints can erode, making movement even more painful and difficult. Inflamed joints can also cause adjacent bones to become either longer or shorter than normal. In some cases, JRA can also affect organs as well as bones.

Is JRA contagious?

No. It's genetic, often passing through several generations before reappearing. Doctors suspect that it may need some environmental "trigger," such as stress or fatigue, to touch it off. It is unusual for more than one child in a family to have it.

Does JRA affect the mind?

No. People with JRA have normal intelligence and personalities.

Is there any cure for JRA?

There is no cure, but with a variety of medications, most of them causing side effects, inflammation can be controlled, pain can be relieved, and joint damage can be prevented or limited.

How do kids with JRA feel about their condition?

As with most serious illnesses, persons with JRA can feel personally hurt by the fact that the illness isn't their fault, that they don't deserve the pain and all the problems. They may blame their parents or resent healthier children, including brothers and sisters. Of course they are especially hurt, emotionally, when people treat them differently or consider them totally incapable of doing things.

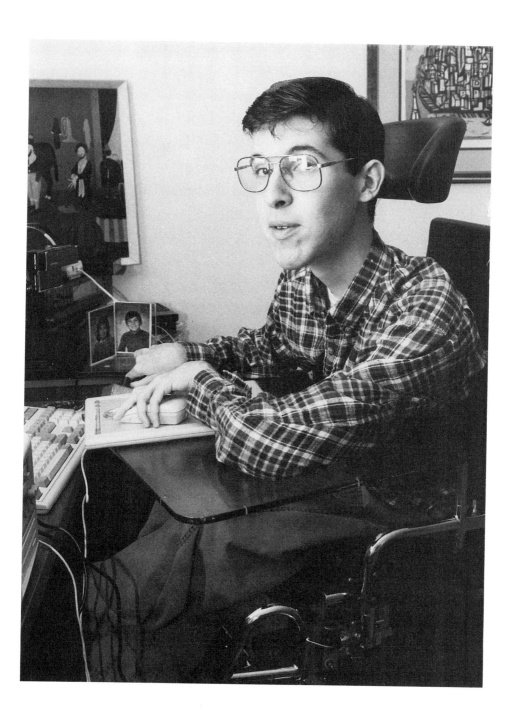

3

Jimmy D'Avanzo

Jimmy's an artist. He has a gift, an eye, a certain talent for creating paintings of striking beauty and surprising juxtapositions of colors and shapes. But his paintings aren't of paint, and he doesn't exactly use a brush. He uses a mouse—the kind that plugs into a computer. With tight, precise movements of his hand, he creates images of things he's seen only in his imagination. In a personal world restricted to the places he can go in a wheelchair, he paints places he creates in his mind.

"I was in nursery school when we realized something was wrong. I couldn't climb stairs anymore. It felt like I had cement shoes. I just couldn't lift my foot up. My parents had me checked for everything. I went through all kinds of tests, and finally it came down to muscular dystrophy (MD). My muscles were deteriorating and didn't work right. Nobody knows the cause of it, and nobody knows a cure. You just keep going downhill, getting weaker and weaker. One day you can't lift up your foot. A couple years later you can't move your leg. A few years later you can't pick up your fork. Right now my lungs can barely cough up fluids.

"Even after the diagnosis I kept going to a regular public school. My mother made sure of that. I wasn't going to be different. But I had to use a walker, and then I had to use leg braces, too. After a while I had to use a wheelchair, and by the sixth grade I couldn't push the wheels anymore, so I got a power wheelchair. That's what I've been using ever since. I can still push the buttons that control it.

"I had friends when I was a kid. My childhood was as normal as it could be under the conditions. I did the same dumb stuff all kids do. Like once we poured antifreeze into a little creek and lit it on fire. Everybody ran off giggling like mad, and I made my getaway in a wheelchair, racing down the street as fast as I could go.

"I stayed in school, but of course kids saw me as different from them. How could they help it? I wore leg braces. I studied at a desk that was high enough for me to stand up at it. When I sat down, the teacher had to lift me up onto my feet while everybody else was standing in line waiting to go to lunch. Of course they looked at me like I was different. That's what kids do.

"One kid was the worst. I don't remember what he called me. 'Weirdo' or something. When my older sister heard about it, she called him up and yelled at him. Then he started rumors about my mother. Never mind exactly what. It was enough to get my sister real mad. I remember seeing her limping down the school corridor looking for him. She'd had knee surgery the day before and the scar had come open. She was limping down the corridor real fast, bleeding at the knee and saying, 'I'm gonna *kill* that kid.' But she didn't, and I guess eventually he grew up enough to be sorry. By the tenth grade he was always offering to help me with things.

"Most people don't say anything obnoxious. They just kind of look at me in a funny way and don't know what to say. My sister says I should let some drool slide down my chin, but I just smile and try to be pleasant.

"What really gets me mad is when a teacher is insensitive or my class schedule gets screwed up. They aren't supposed to give me any classes upstairs, and wouldn't you know, every year they manage to do it. They never think to pull my schedule out of the computer and give it a little personal attention. My mother has to fight them every inch of the way to make the high school building accessible. We aren't asking for anything special, just what the law requires. They finally got the whole school pretty accessible except for one place, the library balcony, and wouldn't you know, they scheduled a class for me right there.

"My mother was at a meeting where all the teachers and the parents of kids with disabilities got together to discuss what the various kids can do, can't do, and really ought to do. After they mentioned all the special treatment I needed, one teacher actually asked why they bothered to go to all that trouble to teach me if I wasn't going to live a normal life span. Of course everybody else came down on him pretty hard, and I bet he was real sorry he said it, but you've got to wonder how anybody could be so insensitive.

"In junior high school I couldn't get down to the cafeteria, so they brought lunch to me in a classroom. A bunch of kids would come eat with me. We had a regular fraternity. It was great. We didn't feel cut off. We felt special.

"But MD sure stunts your social life. You get to be very reclusive. It's just too much to overcome. I mean, besides all the normal teenage problems of personality and trying to fit in, there's the physical problem. You end up not having many friends at all. You stay home all the time and can't go out unless somebody in the family takes you.

"And that creates its own problems. I mean, I'm *always* here. Every time somebody in the family turns around, here I am. I can't get away from them, and they can't get away from me. It can drive you crazy. In the back of my mind I'm always kind of bitter about my condition, and there's nobody to blame but the people around me, which of course I don't mean to, but there they are. I kind of get out of control, yelling stuff that doesn't even make sense. Thank God my parents are able to deal with me when I get into those moods. Not that I believe in God. I mean, I go to church every Sunday because it makes my mother happy, but I can't believe a God would make so many problems for people. Not just for me. I mean all over the world.

"I think one of the most frustrating things for me is that I can't return any of the help my family gives me. There's no way I can show gratitude. I can't say, 'Hey, Dad, I'll go mow the lawn for you.' I don't know if I'd say that anyway, but it would be nice if I could. My mom says I treat her like a slave, but what can I do? She's just kidding, but it's true. Whatever I need, just a glass of water or something, I have to ask for it. I can't even lift my arms.

"I can't wash my own face, and I can't get up in the morning and take a shower without help. When I take a shower, which I get to do only every other day, all I can do is sit there in a chair. I can't adjust the temperature, can't do anything. It's nice to just sit there and let the water pour down, but sometimes I wish I could just get up in the morning and take a cold shower. It would help me wake up.

"I've been to support groups where people with all kinds of disabilities sit around and gripe about how hard life is. I never got into it at all until one day somebody was talking about alienation, how you get cut off from the world because you've got physical problems. He talked about other kids teasing him. That touched me. When I heard that I related to it and knew I wasn't the only one. I also knew that, yeah, I can deal with it.

"This summer my parents hired a college kid to take me around. He was real nice. He got to be a regular part of the family. We'd go down to the mall or whatever. He helped me get to a summer job I had, doing artwork on a computer. But then he got a real job, so off he goes, and I have to find somebody else. I start college next week, and I need somebody to take me to class, set up my computer, and then to take notes for me. I just hope I can remember to speak up for myself. It's too easy to just let whoever's standing there take charge and make decisions and tell people what I'm supposed to be telling them.

"A big moment in my life was in the tenth grade

when I got to study computer art. It opened a new door. It was something I could do. I'd never thought I was good at art before because I couldn't really hold a pencil or a brush. But with the computer, just by rolling the mouse around, I could choose a kind of brush, a particular shade of color, and I could draw something just as well as anyone could do with a real brush. I did it better than other kids, and I did it well enough to see myself really producing art. I entered a national computer art contest at high school level and took one of the higher awards. It wasn't a contest for people with disabilities or anything. They couldn't see the predicament I'm in. They just saw my art.

"I don't know what it is about art or why it means so much to me. I have a kind of gift. I don't know where it comes from. It's a kind of vision. It's connected to physical disability, but I don't know how. It's something about how your attitude changes.

"When my mother saw an article in the paper about a local artist whose computer art was being shown in New Haven, she called her up and asked her to come see me. Now she's kind of taken me under her wing. She showed me how you can do real art on a computer. We worked together on two articles about computer graphics software. She analyzed the Mac version and I did the DOS version. Two of my works have been in computer magazines. She comes over to the house every month or so and gives me ideas and suggestions.

"I heard about this artist who was already pretty famous when he was in an accident or something and was paralyzed. Now he can't move his arms or legs. Now he has to paint using a brush in his mouth. And his paintings are still good. You couldn't tell the difference between before the accident and after. One thing he said really impressed me. He said, 'I'd paint if I had to spit it onto the canvas.' That's the kind of artist I am. I have to do it. It's part of me.

"Next week I start college. I'm going to major in art. I've already met the guy in charge of the art department. He's cool. There's something about people in art. They're a little looser. They can see past the physical part of things. They're more willing to accept differences.

"That's what I want to do in life. My biggest dream is to become an artist known all over the world. I want people to look at my art and think, 'Wow, he's incredible.'"

Questions about Muscular Dystrophy

What is muscular dystrophy?

There is no single disease called muscular dystrophy. The term refers to a group of hereditary disorders that destroy muscle tissues. Some attack motor nerve cells in the spinal cord. Others cause failure in the transmission of signals from nerves to muscles. Others cause chemical deficiencies. The result is a muscle weakness that gets worse. Usually, symptoms begin during childhood or adolescence. Life span is usually shortened substantially.

Are people with muscular dystrophy mentally disabled?

No. Only their muscles, often including facial muscles and eyes, are affected. Their brains and personalities remain normal.

What should I say if I meet someone with muscular dystrophy?

Say the same thing you'd say to anyone else. Offer whatever help seems appropriate to the situation (opening a door, picking something up, etc.). People with MD might be offended if you cater to them too much, but a polite offer and an acceptance of "No thanks" is quite appropriate.

4

Lori Siedman

Lori Siedman loves to talk. She's in the eighth grade and loves getting together with her friends so everybody can wiggle their hands at each other. It's a silent conversation of signs, but if Lori's there, it touches off bursts of laughter. Big problem: too much time spent using the phone, which takes a little longer than usual because she's got to type whatever she wants to say. She likes her friends so much she'd rather go to school than stay home. Like just about every other fourteen-year-old, she loves Italian food, hopes to go to college somewhere out of state, and is dying to get away and be on her own.

"I was deaf when I was born. For about a year, no one knew why. When I was about eleven, my mother noticed I was having trouble seeing. I bumped into things a lot at home and at school and had trouble finding little things I

39

dropped. If I wasn't looking right at the thing, I couldn't see it. The eye doctor tested me and found out I had almost no vision around the sides of my eyes. It's as if I'm always looking through two tiny pinholes. They call this problem Usher syndrome, which was also the cause of my deafness. It's genetic. It makes you deaf and then, little by little, blind.

"I was in the sixth grade when I found out I had Usher syndrome. My mother tried to explain it with sign language, but I didn't really understand. She was trying to explain *retinitis pigmentosa*, which is the degeneration of the retina. Then my counselor at school explained it, and I knew what it meant. I was shocked and got really mad. It just wasn't fair.

"When I was younger, I believed in God, but when I found out I had Usher syndrome, I became an atheist. I didn't think God would do such a thing to me or have bad things happen to so many people in the world or let bad people have it so good. I'm Jewish, but I don't go to synagogue because there are no interpreters in my hometown or nearby towns. We celebrate Hanukkah and Rosh Hashanah, but we also have a Christmas tree. Technically, it's Dave's Christmas tree. He's my stepfather; he's a Catholic.

"I stopped being an atheist recently when I went to a Youth Group meeting at a neighborhood church. The youth leaders there and my hearing friend explained why I should believe in God. My friends told me God had come into their hearts, and some said God had come into their bedrooms. Through the interpreter, I told the youth leaders that God had never come into my heart or my bedroom. When I went to a second meeting there, the youth leaders gave me a Bible. I started reading it and little by little, I started believing that there is a God, and I began to pray.

"My parents got divorced when I was five. I was really sad about that. My mother married Dave a few years later. I get to see my father three times a week. He's going to get married later, so then I'll have a stepmother and also a stepsister, which will be nice because I've never had a sister before, or a brother.

"I go to a school for deaf children. I really like it. I love to use sign language. I have so many friends there. We talk and talk and talk, always joking around and having a good time. We get so crazy. There's a whole deaf culture that hearing people don't know about. I love to meet deaf people. I don't have any best friend, but I have a lot of good friends.

"Some of the kids get to live at the school. I wish I did. They have such a good time in the dorm. I get to stay there on Tuesday and Thursday nights to socialize and to have tutor sessions. Maybe next year I'll get to live there. I sure would like to. It's a lot better than staying at home.

"At my school we have three kids with Usher syndrome—me and a junior and a senior. We meet once a week with my counselor, to talk about how we deal with the syndrome. I also hold workshops for other people to teach them about the syndrome and my eye problem. A person who works at the Board of Education Services for the Blind taught the other kids what it's like by letting them look through some special glasses that let you see only what people with Usher syndrome see. The glasses are cardboard with just pinholes in front of the eyes. When the kids looked through the glasses, they were nervous. They knew how it feels.

"I can't wait till I graduate! I want to go to any college for deaf people, the farther away the better, and then go out and get a job. But graduation isn't till five years from now. I wish it was tomorrow.

"I like math and history, but I hate science and English. I don't like vocational skills because I don't like working with machines. I'd rather work with people. And when I get a job, I'd rather not work with machines, not even a computer. I don't know what my major's going to be in college, and I don't know what kind of career I'm going to have. I'll decide about that when I'm a junior or a senior. Right now I couldn't care less. I go to school because it's so much fun. I hate it when school's canceled because of bad weather. There's nothing to do at home.

"I can't listen to music because I can't hear it unless it's loud enough to feel the vibrations. I've never heard music. I don't know why people like it. I think maybe it's just because they like the person who's singing it. They think the singer's wonderful, so they think the music is, too.

"It's funny; some kids at my school walk around using a little cassette player with earphones. They can't even hear it! The most they can do is feel the vibrations against their ears, enough to feel the beat but not really hear the music. I think they do it just because they want to be like all the kids who can hear. They just want to fit in.

"I don't know how to talk except for a few words that sound weird to people. Some deaf people learn to talk, but it depends on how great their hearing loss is and on their speech training. Right now, when I'm with hearing people, I can't hear what they are talking about, and even if I could, I couldn't talk to them unless they knew American Sign Language. I don't know many people who aren't deaf or don't know any sign language. When I'm with hearing people, I just get kind of puzzled. I don't know what's going on. In a situation like that, I just sit back and think about something else.

"Being deaf isn't something you can see. I mean, if somebody who doesn't know me sees me, they think I can hear. If they say something to me, I won't even notice unless I see their lips, and because I can see only out of the center of my eyes, I'd have to be looking right at their lips. Once I figure out they're talking to me, all I can do is point to my ear and shake my head. Sometimes they understand; sometimes they don't. Sometimes they try to use gestures to make me understand, sometimes they just ignore me, and sometimes they run away. I don't mind using gestures if they want to, but it can get boring. I think everybody should learn sign language. There's a lot of deaf people in the world.

"I can usually make myself understood by gesturing. If I'm in a restaurant, I just point to the menu. If I go to McDonalds or something, they figure things out fast enough.

"One day my mother stayed in the car and sent me into the store to buy milk. I was standing behind a lady. I thought she was talking to herself. She just kept speaking and speaking and speaking. So I pointed to my ear and shook my head. She spoke again and again and again. She pointed to the cash register and the counter. I stared at her lips but just couldn't understand her. Then she took my jug of milk and put it on the counter and walked around behind me. She was letting me go ahead of her in the line because she had a lot of things and I had only a jug of milk.

"My mother gets mad at me when I'm on the phone too long. We have a little computer called a TTY. With it I can connect to another deaf person's TTY by the telephone and we can type to each other. If I want to talk with a hearing person, I can call a company called the Relay Center and they call the person I want to talk to. Then I type what I want to say, and the Relay operator reads the message to the other person. Then that person talks and the operator types it so I can read it. It's a good way to chat on the phone, but it takes a long time. Since I love to talk, we end up with a huge phone bill and the phone's always busy.

"Usually I can only call local people. Most of my friends are from other towns, so I spend my day doing homework, writing stories, reading books, playing computer games, and watching TV. Sometimes I get depressed because I don't have many friends near where I live. And it's depressing to have Usher syndrome.

"I'm not sure how life will be when I grow up and live on my own. I know I have to learn to do things by myself, but there will always be things I can't do. And before too long, I'll be completely blind. Then I don't know what I'll do. They have computers that can talk to blind people, even read a book to them, but that doesn't help if you're deaf. Neither does sign language if you're blind. I just don't know what I'm going to do. I don't even want to think about it. I just hope scientists find a way to prevent blindness or slow it down so when I get older, I can still see."

Questions about Deafness and Usher Syndrome

How would I know if I was catching Usher syndrome?

Usher syndrome is not contagious, so you can't catch it. It's genetic. The first indication is deafness or hearing impairment at or shortly after birth.

Usher syndrome in the United States is estimated to occur in about one in 15,000 to 30,000 births. About 3 percent of cases of profound deafness are caused by it, and it is the most common cause of deaf-blindness. There is no known cure for it.

How are people who are deaf different from other people?

The only difference is that they can't hear. Deaf people lead normal lives, drive cars, hold jobs, and have families. Like everyone else, they want to be part of society and do the things everyone else does.

Why do some people with hearing impairments sound funny when they talk?

They may never have heard speech. The way people learn to speak is by hearing those around them. If they can't hear (or hear well), the only way they can learn to speak is by being taught to move their mouth into various positions. Of course it's almost impossible to do so in precisely the same way as people who can hear, so even the most capable will sound like they have a foreign accent.

What should I do if I start talking to someone who turns out to be deaf?

The person may be able to read your lips, though not perfectly. That, combined with gestures, may be enough to get your message across. The best way to communicate would be to write things, even if only with your finger forming letters on your palm.

Is it hard to learn sign language?

Just as with any other language, learning American Sign Language (ASL) takes practice, and you need to use it to get good at it. If you know anyone who is deaf, it would be very nice to learn to talk with that person. You should also learn a few key signs that would be useful in your job or in common situations with strangers. Some good ones to learn would be "Please," "Thank you," "Hello," "Can I help you?," "What would you like?," and so on.

Here are a few signs worth learning. You can find more in a library (look under "Deafness" or "American

Sign Language") or by contacting the National Association of the Deaf or the Retina Pigmentosa Foundation, which are listed in the "Resources" section of this book.

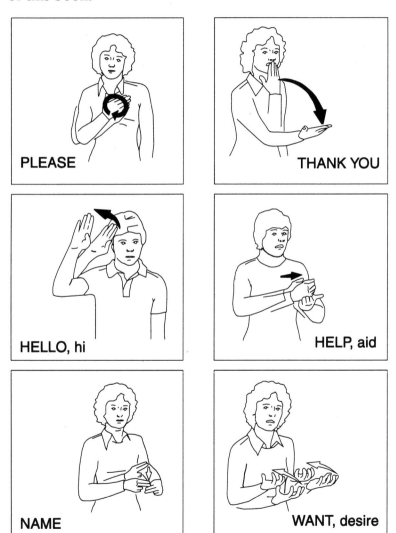

PLEASE

THANK YOU

HELLO, hi

HELP, aid

NAME

WANT, desire

5

Nate Barnes

Nate lives in a rough neighborhood in a rough city, but he's built himself a paradise of sound. Though he just turned eighteen, he's already an accomplished musician, touring the country with gospel groups. If you wandered into his bedroom, you'd think you'd stumbled into a bizarre music studio overgrown with drums, electronic keyboards, recording equipment, and speakers. Styling himself after such musicians as Sigmund Morriar, Stanley Brown, and Gerald Haywater, he's creating his own style of gospel-funk-jazz. By some kind of miracle, he's managing to rise up from his rough surroundings even though he hasn't seen a thing since he turned eleven. Somehow he's managed to turn an overwhelming obstacle into a stepping stone.

"I went blind because of weak retinas. Those are the linings on the inside of the eyeball, the part that's sensitive to light. When it happened, I didn't think much about it. It didn't seem to matter. I kind of knew it was going to happen because it came on gradually. In the summer after the third grade, a couple weeks after my birthday, I had an operation. My eyes were swollen for a while, and I thought that's why I couldn't see. Then the doctor told me I was blind and there was nothing they could do about it. But it didn't seem to matter to me. It was another day in my life. I went home and just hung around outside. All the other kids were playing, and I was hanging around not seeing anything.

"Nothing really changed for me. Maybe my mother spoiled me a little, but not much and not for long. I still got punished the same as always. I was on the wrong track before I went blind, and I still was. Ever since I was about ten, most of my friends were teenagers. Until I couldn't see, we were always stealing stuff, vandalizing, harassing people, sneaking around on roofs, and doing stuff that was dangerous. My teachers didn't like me because I talked back and wouldn't pay attention. I was worse than the average kid. The teachers were always telling me, 'Don't you come back to school without your mother or your uncle.' They knew my father didn't live with us and that my uncle was a teacher, so they wanted to talk with him. But of course I never brought him.

"I thought I'd accepted my blindness, but now,

looking back on it, I see that deep, deep, deep, *deep* inside, I was mad. In the fourth and fifth grades, I did even worse in school. Sometimes I got so depressed I just wouldn't go for a week. About the only thing that mattered to me was my music. It was always there for me. I kind of knew my life was going to be tied around music, but of course I wasn't doing anything about it. Every once in a while I asked if I could have a drum set, but I didn't actually *beg* for one. Besides, my mother was very ill at the time. She had an aneurysm in her brain and almost died. No way she was going to spend money on a drum set.

"When I started doing bad in the sixth grade, they sent me to a school in a nice suburb north of the city where my uncle taught. I was totally depressed at the time. Inside, I knew I was going to be somebody someday, but I felt like my whole life had already wasted away because I was already in the sixth grade.

"Basically, I flunked the sixth grade. Things looked really bad for me. But then a teacher sat down with me and explained that being so depressed wasn't doing anybody any good. I wasn't doing myself or my mother any good. He said that if I wanted to make music my life, and if I wanted to make my mother proud, then I had to get back on my feet and start doing it.

"And that turned me right around. Nobody was

helping more than my mother, so I wasn't going to let her down. Ever since then I've been forming a better view of what I want to do in life. In the seventh grade, my grades started to get better. I started practicing drums at the church. I didn't have a teacher so I was teaching myself. My Uncle Stanley convinced everybody to get me some drums. I was fourteen when I got my first set.

"I was practically brought up in church, so that's where my music started. I owe a lot to Kenny Moales, the pastor there. He got me playing gospel, and I started mixing in jazz and funk. It became the most important thing in my life because I loved it and could do it better than other people. My church, Prayer Tabernacle Church of Love, had a big gospel group, and I started playing drums for them. Pretty soon we were traveling every weekend and playing for other groups, like the Connecticut Choral Union and Greater Love. This summer, I've been home only one week and one weekend. The rest of the time, I'm on tour. I was in Chicago last week and before that in South Carolina and Virginia and Boston.

"My main attraction to music at first was the money, but now I love the music on top of that. It's so much a part of me. It's one of those things that helped me get through this ordeal. It was like a security blanket, something I could always fall back on. It was a way to get people not to feel sorry for me. You can't let people start feeling sorry for you or pretty soon they're doing everything for you, and that only makes things worse. You never learn to do things for yourself.

"People respect me because of my music. I go to Warren Harding High School. It's a pretty tough place, but I get around. Nobody messes with me. I'm shy, so I always had trouble making friends. But lately, you wouldn't believe how many people are hanging around with me. I've figured out that people feel more comfortable around me when I joke about my blindness. I say something like, 'Hey, did you see *that!*' and everybody laughs. Humor shortens the process of them seeing how I'm just like everybody else.

"But it seems like a lot of people are scared of me because I'm blind, like I'm some kind of weird thing they don't know how to deal with. It's like they think they have to treat me different. And then I feel like I *am* different. I try to blend with everybody, but some people make me feel like I'm standing out. I'm always worried I'm wearing the wrong clothes or something.

"I get such *stupid* questions! Like, 'How do you go to the bathroom?' I'm like, 'what do they think?' What's blind got to do with it? Some people just don't use their brains.

"I go to the same classes as everybody else. Either I

get around by myself or a teacher or friend or my girlfriend helps me. The only thing different I do is study Braille. Braille's like a foreign language. You have to practice all the time and keep on going to class every day. There's so many rules and regulations you have to memorize. One symbol can mean five or six different things depending on what it comes after and where in a sentence it's at. But you can learn it if you try, and it's important. I got to thank my Braille teacher, John Wargo, who's been teaching me since the third grade.

"Sometimes I feel trapped because I can't do something if somebody doesn't help me. But then I think, even if you *aren't* blind, you're *still* always going to need help.

"I feel like I've got my life very much under control. It looks like I'm going to get into the Berklee College of Music in Boston with a full scholarship. They've got people from all over the world studying music there. They're already sending a teacher to give me lessons once a week. It's the first time I've had a drum teacher. I'm also learning keyboard. Right now I'm working on my own arrangement of 'Für Elise,' by Beethoven. A friend of mine lets me use his sound studio, so I play keyboard on one track, then can go back and accompany myself on drums. Later this year I'm going to be cutting two records with a gospel group, and next year another one in Cincinnati.

"Opportunity's knocking on so many doors! It's all happening so fast. My only problem is figuring out which doors to open. I know I'm going to be somebody someday. I just want to be mentally prepared for it. I don't want to forget where I came from. This city used to be so great, with factories and jobs and stores everywhere, but they let it all waste away. The factories are gone and the stores are boarded up. If you saw my neighborhood, you'd think it was in a nice suburb somewhere. But if you walk a couple blocks to a main avenue, everything's filthy. 'Cause of all the shoot-outs between drug dealers, I'm afraid to walk over there and catch a bus. If they start shooting, I can't run fast enough to find shelter.

"Today all those kids I used to hang out with are so strung out on dope I can hardly talk to them. It's like they're completely different people. I'm the only one who didn't go bad. So sometimes I *thank God* for sending me blindness. It saved me.

"Blindness also taught me to be more observant. Eyes are only one way of seeing. You also see with your other senses. Now I use them more. I can judge people better now just by listening, by asking questions and hearing how they respond. I pay keen attention to people. That's one of the qualities of a better person.

"If I knew somebody who just went blind, I'd say, 'Don't let your blindness overcome you. Don't let it be an obstacle. Go for it. Overcome it. Obstacles are meant to step over or go around. It's not easy. You're going to have a lot of rough stones in your path. One of them is envy. People are going to envy you when they see you doing something better than them.' This summer when I was in a special program for young musicians from all over the world, I had drummers come up and challenge me. Some of them were older than me. They just had to show me how they were better, which actually they weren't. But they just couldn't accept that. They didn't know that you can learn from everybody, whether they're better than you or worse. There's always something else to learn, but some people just can't get that through their heads. They can't *see*."

Questions about Blindness

When and how should I offer help to a blind person?

Blind people are generally able to get around and take care of themselves. If they seem to be getting along well, there's no need to offer help. If they seem lost, confused, or about to walk into danger, an offer of help would probably be appreciated.

To offer help, first say something so they know you're there. Don't suddenly grab them without warning.

How should I walk with a blind person?

Let him or her hold your arm and walk normally. You might warn the person of steps, curbs, or hazards coming up, but there's usually no need to slow down or take special precautions. He or she will probably let you keep about half a step ahead. Don't push the person ahead of you or try to steer from behind.

How can I talk with a blind person without saying something offensive like, "Do you see what I mean?" or "Look what I found?"

Don't worry about using words like "look" and "see." After all, those words mean more than just visual perception. Just talk normally. An awkward, artificial remark like "Touch what I found" doesn't make anybody feel better.

Is Braille hard to learn?

It isn't much harder than learning to read visually. It takes six months to a year to get good at it, and then, like anything else, it depends on practice. Braille uses six raised dots to form the letters of the alphabet and also several "contractions," which are common phrases reduced to a single set of dots.

Modern computers can actually scan typewritten pages and read them out loud, but without Braille, a blind person is virtually illiterate. In the absence of a computer, he or she would not be able to read.

Do blind people always have extra sharp hearing?

If blind people have normal hearing abilities, they will probably learn to interpret sounds better than sighted people, and they may pay more attention to sounds. Very often, however, the cause of blindness may have caused hearing problems, as well.

6

Andi Nordstrom

Andi Nordstrom is an exceptionally pretty girl whose Scandinavian blonde hair of childhood is turning a reddish brown. Before her accident, she used to like to draw and paint, and sometimes she thinks maybe she'd like to write a book. She likes to look into Oriental philosophy a bit, then maybe read some science fiction or a play by Oscar Wilde, who happens to have the same name as her cat. Her parents are divorced, and both have remarried. She has lived with both of them, first in Wisconsin, then in North Carolina, then back to Wisconsin, and it looks like she's going back to North Carolina. Basically, those are her two choices. There isn't much she can do about it.

"Oh, how I wish I could go back and change the events on that day in the middle of September in North Carolina. But then who knows, I may have stayed stupid.

A friend and I decided we'd head to the beach after school. I was hoping to see a boy I liked surfing there. Several days before, I had told my old boyfriend I wasn't interested in him anymore. We caught a ride with some guys we sort of knew but could care less about. We had no idea of how we were going to get home.

"When we got to the beach, the boy I had a crush on was surfing with a friend. For a while we hung around watching them, laughing at their spills, and smoking cigarettes. My friend then went off with another girl to smoke some pot. They invited me, but I declined, not for angelic reasons but because I hated the high and how it would make me act like a giggling idiot without control of myself. I hate being out of control. I was feeling fine enough. Until my ex-boyfriend showed up.

"He didn't come up to me, and I did my best to show him I didn't care if he dropped dead. I was tired of his immaturity. Thankfully, he left a few minutes later.

"After a while, I started glancing nervously at my watch. I was supposed to be home by dinnertime on school days. If I'd had any money on me, I would have called my mother or stepfather, but I'd spent my lunch money on cigarettes. I had to wait until the two boys were done surfing. Twenty-five cents could have saved me from a nightmare.

"Five of us rode in the car, a beat-up four-door

Dodge Omni. The boy I liked was driving. His friend was in the other front seat; my friend, the girl she smoked pot with, and I were in back. I sat behind the driver. As usual, I locked my car door because I had always had a fear of doors flying open and me falling out.

"We stopped by my ex-boyfriend's house to get some things the driver had left there back when they were good friends. An argument broke out between them, so when we left we were being driven by a very angry driver. We got out on the highway, he was going too fast, and his driving was erratic. At one point he threw one of our textbooks out the window. We all yelled at him to slow down, but he didn't listen.

"Suddenly, he raced up behind a slow car and had to dodge onto the shoulder to avoid hitting it. The shoulder was soft and sandy. When he tried to turn back onto the road, the tire caught the pavement and flipped the car. We went airborne, then hit the earth and tumbled a few hundred feet before hitting a utility box and going airborne again. Sometime during all of this, the driver and I were thrown out of the car. It would be forty minutes before an ambulance arrived.

"I don't remember any of this. I just woke up in a hospital room, my head fixed in place by two steel pins. Tubes went up into my nose, and a respirator was breathing for me through a tube that went in through a hole in my trachea. A TV was tuned into the Smurfs. Almost a week had passed.

"I was told that I had been in a car wreck and had broken my neck. Neither this nor the fact that all I could move was my left arm slightly bothered me. They had me doped up on morphine. I couldn't speak because of the trachea incision, so I mouthed words asking about the others in the car. All were fine except the driver, who had died of massive head injuries.

"The doctors at that hospital had no experience with spinal cord injury, so I had to be flown to the Shepherd Spinal Center in Atlanta. My mother told me I would be there for three months. My heart filled with despair. Three months! A lifetime away from my home and friends, such a long time before I could begin walking again.

"As I was carried on a stretcher to the helicopter, I could feel myself getting sick but I fought it back. I just couldn't let myself throw up in a helicopter! A voice somewhere told me that we were going for a little ride and that everything was going to be okay.

"In a haze of painkillers and nausea, I heard the propeller blades start moving. For some reason I imagined myself raising my hand up into the blades. I guess I fell asleep after that. I remember nothing more until a drizzly rain misted over my face as they took me out of the helicopter in Atlanta.

"The special care unit of Shepherd Spinal Center had no individual rooms, just one very large room with many beds separated by curtains. I didn't like that at all. Nurses hooked me up to a respirator, made sure my lungs were relatively free of fluid, and did all the other things they do with a new patient. When they asked me how I was feeling, I mouthed the word 'fine,' but I was lying. I was desperate to throw up. Looking back, I realize I was putting myself in danger. Had I thrown up when no one was near, I could have drowned in my own vomit. For some strange reason I decided to wait until my mother arrived. But the drive for her to Atlanta would be over five hours. When she finally arrived, she held up a small basin and helped me turn my head. I threw up dark green liquid. It was the first sign that things weren't going to get better.

"Over the next week, they figured out that my digestive system had shut down. I had to have a hard plastic tube put into my nose and down my throat into my stomach to drain away the built-up fluid. The pain of the tube being forced up into my nose was agonizing. I heard crackling noises and thought for sure my nose was slowly being broken from the inside. Had I a voice, I would have screamed.

67

"Next I developed a large blood clot in the left side of my neck, an extremely deadly situation. At the same time, I got pneumonia and a fever sometimes reaching 106 degrees. The doctors decided that the apparatus fixed into my trachea was too small, that it was meant for a child, and so they exchanged it for a larger one. Up until this point, the most pain I'd ever experienced was from the tube in my nose, but that had been nothing compared to the pain I felt this time. With no anesthesia, a doctor pulled the old tube out of the hole in the front of my throat and put in a new one. It cannot be done gently. It has to be forced. The pain was excruciating. Now I know what it feels like to have your throat literally ripped open. They would do this two more times before my hospital stay was through.

"Depression was setting in, and I was becoming addicted to painkillers. I lay awake at night, waiting for the three hours to be up so I could get my next dose. I was on a bed that slowly tilted from side to side so I wouldn't get bedsores. When the bed tilted to the right, I could see out the window into the nurses' station. When it tilted to the left, I could see the get-well cards taped up on my wall and the monitors for my heart and breathing.

"This was a mournful time for me. I couldn't think past the next shot of painkillers. I didn't think about getting out of there some day. Life was a routine of sleep interrupted by pain, fear, and craving.

"The rehabilitation place concentrated on three areas: physical rehab, occupational rehab, and psychological rehab. Physical rehab started with just having me in a chair and not in bed. Therapists moved my arms and legs around to keep them limber. They try to get you as strong as you can be to do as much as you can, even if it's just lifting your head and shifting yourself around while lying down. Then there was mat work where they propped me up on my arms, leaning back on them while I lay there. It was extremely painful, as though my arms were going to shoot up through my shoulders. I would beg for them to get me off my arms, but they would say, 'Just a few more minutes, Andi.'

"Occupational therapy involves strengthening your arms and teaching you how to do as much as you can with whatever control you have left in your hands and arms. They customize holding devices for you depending on your need. They taught me how to feed myself, brush my teeth, draw and stuff by using splints or special holding devices.

"Psychological therapy involved group therapy where we told others how we came to be in the position we were in and discussed our fears and tried to help others with their pain. There were also individual sessions with psychologists. I guess there were some sessions where my parents talked with the counselors, but I would never have known it if one psychiatrist hadn't mentioned that my father started to cry when told that there was no reason why I couldn't still have children.

"I was having great difficulty doing things I had always taken for granted before. Still, I thought for sure I'd be one of the few lucky ones who walked away from their injury. I couldn't help thinking that since I could wiggle my toes, I would someday be able to move my legs enough to walk on them. My spinal cord injury, which was at the third and fourth cervical vertebrae, was an incomplete injury. The entire spinal cord wasn't severed. This meant that I had some control over my arms at least, but not my hands or legs. They told me I might improve a little, but there would be no miracle for me.

"When I finally came home, nobody knew what to do with me. Before that, I had always liked to draw and had wanted to be an artist. Now I found little joy in drawing with pencils attached to my wrist splints. I couldn't move my hands, fingers, or my wrists. I had a little control over my left arm, but it would be a while before I gained just a little control over my right. To draw, I had to maneuver my shoulder to make my wrist move the pencil. It just didn't work. I ended up just reading or watching TV.

"I manage to do things like eat, brush my teeth, and type by having utensils attached to my wrist splints. I can't lift an arm over my head or pick something up off the floor. I have to sleep on my back all night. I'd give anything to be able to roll over and slip my hands under my pillow. But I'm thankful I have at least some control. I can bend my legs a little, sit myself up a bit and sort of flex my wrists. It could have been worse.

"When I got home from the hospital, my best friend came to see me, the one who was with me in the car accident. But after seven months of not seeing each other and her being a messed-up person to begin with, the friendship died on the spot. I haven't seen her since.

"My ex-boyfriend also stopped by, unannounced. He had visited me in the hospital several times. I'd totally forgotten that I had broken up with him until one night the memory came back to me. From that point on, my hate for him festered. I was sitting there in the kitchen when he came in. It killed me to have this jerk looking down at me in a wheelchair. I took one look at him and told him to get out. My older sister said she had never seen me treat anybody so coldly.

"That summer it was decided I should spend the summer with my father and stepmother in Milwaukee, Wisconsin, where I was born and grew up.

"I was very nervous when I got off the plane in

Milwaukee because my little half-sister, who was ten, hadn't seen me after the accident. I was afraid that she'd fall apart at seeing her older sister in a wheelchair. She took in the sight of me quietly and gravely without the fake smiles and cheerful greetings that adults feel necessary.

"When we got to my father's house—the house I grew up in—I was suddenly devastated. They'd built a ramp up the front steps to the porch. That's when the reality of it hit me.

"My stepmother and I started out on good terms, which was a big relief. When I was littler, I was always afraid of her. But when I arrived in a wheelchair, she said she was glad to have me there and if I needed anything, all I had to do was ask. She and my father hired a girl to help me with my exercises, fix lunch, and do whatever else I needed. Her name was Debbie, and we got along quite well. But over the course of the summer, my stepmother took a disliking to her and accused her of neglecting my two sisters. Soon Debbie quit because hostilities got to be too much. The next day my stepmother tried to take over my exercises—moving my arms around to keep the muscles and tendons loose—but I resisted by just not cooperating in the least.

"My stepmother's goodwill and benevolence were short-lived. Her temper is still short and fierce, and I never know what will set it off. Now I'm more helpless than I was as a child. I'm afraid the way I was when I was little. Even though my bedroom is a sunroom just off the kitchen, to me it is a dark cell, a miserable place of banishment and retreat.

"Sometimes when she's real mad about something and has to help me get dressed, she snaps at me through gritted teeth. She gets crazy ideas and accuses me of things like plotting to ruin her marriage with my father so that my mother could marry him again. I've given up trying to defend myself because I'd just set her off. One time I asked her to stop because she was scaring me. I thought that might make her realize what she was doing, but all she said was 'Good.'

"Nothing can kill your pride more quickly than having to depend on someone. The worst part is having no control over yourself. All I can do is surrender. I don't talk back and I don't defend myself, but in my mind I know she wouldn't treat me this way if I could get out of this chair.

"In the middle of all this, my father just goes on living in his own world. I think he has a lot of anger and resentment towards me. He's a big man with a powerful voice and ever since I was little I've always been intimidated into submission. When he yells at me, I get so mad and frustrated that I cry, and then he tells me to quit bawling. (My lungs were left weakened by my accident. I don't make a sound when I cry.) He yells at me for getting in that car accident. He makes like I'm a terrible person because I used to smoke cigarettes, drink beer, and skip so much school that I failed a grade, all of which added up to me being paralyzed and inflicting myself on the family.

"Part of me knows they have no reason to be saying this stuff about me. I mean, I could have slipped in the bathtub and ended up the same way. But they still think nothing would have stopped me from self-destruction except having my neck broken. I'll never be able to disprove them. No matter what I do, I'm still that lousy kid who spent her lunch money on cigarettes and got into the wrong car.

"And maybe they've got some reason to treat me this way. I mean, like, sometimes I just get so frustrated at having to ask for everything to be done. Sometimes I forget that they're hurt and frustrated, too. I can sound like I just expect them to wait on me, hand and foot. And of course they tell me that, too, just to make sure I feel bad about it. You have to be a real diplomat if you're paralyzed. You have to ask for things in just the right way and at just the right time. You can't do it if they're in a bad mood or if they just sat down. If I ask for something in the wrong tone of voice, I have to hear how I'm selfish and thankless.

"When I lived with my mother, she always let me express myself. I could talk back if I felt like it, and yes, there had been times when I called her some nasty things and swore at her. But she never punished me or forbade me to speak out. I've always respected her for that. She let me control myself and my thoughts. But since I came to live with my father, I've lost this right. When you can't even leave the room, and can't defend yourself verbally, you have nothing.

"I remember the first time I saw the bus that was to take me to school. I was totally humiliated. It was the same bus that carried the mentally handicapped kids. When I was in grade school, whenever any of us kids saw one of the handicapped buses pass by, we'd elbow whoever was beside us and say 'There goes your bus.'

"Now the bus stops for me. At first I was the only passenger. But now we pick up other kids, all of whom are so mentally incapacitated that they hardly know where they are. One of them whimpers all the time, and one of them looks like an old bum. One girl pulls her hair out and bangs her head against the side of the bus, yelling 'No!' each time. It makes a sickening sound. I have to sit there with them and watch it all. I don't have anything against these poor kids, but I keep thinking,

'You are judged by the company you keep.' And there I sit, and there's nothing in the world I can do about it.

"Thank God that's only on the bus. During the school day I go to regular classes. But I don't have any real friends, only associates. So I keep them at arm's length and for the first time in my life, I just concentrate on my schoolwork. Never did I ever even dream that I'd get on the honor roll much less the merit roll. Somehow, my family doesn't seem to notice this change.

"Books are my only escape. With a good book I can forget that I can't walk, that my friends have abandoned me, that each school day is a day of humiliation. Sometimes I truly wish to die. Yes, every day since that accident, I have thought about death. Of course, unless I come across a convenient cliff, it's physically impossible for me to kill myself. And even if I could, I don't think that I could do it. It would hurt my family too much. I have to live."

Questions about Paralysis

How do quadriplegics and paraplegics feel about their situation?

They tend to go through stages, though not always in any particular order. Depression is inevitable and very often leads to thoughts of suicide. Victims may go through a stage of asking "Why me?" and "What is the purpose of life?" When they first come home from rehabilitation, depression can worsen. As victim and family try to deal with the increased difficulties, frustration can lead to anger. The victim may feel undesirable or useless. As the person develops capabilities, finds new friends, and goes back to school or work, the depression and anger can build toward a readjustment of values and a strong degree of pride and self-esteem.

Victims of spinal injury, amputation, and traumatic head injury often learn a lot about themselves by talking with people with similar problems. Support groups are often a big help.

What's the difference between a quadriplegic and a paraplegic?

The quadriplegic has lost all or most control of muscles in the arms and legs. The paraplegic has lost control of muscles below the waist. They may or may not retain tactile sensation in those areas.

How can friends help?

In cases where the victim's lifestyle led to the accident, the new lifestyle may lead to a whole new set of friends. Friends, old or new, should remember that paralysis does not affect the person inside the body. He or she is still going to want to keep busy, have fun, go out, talk, and so on.

In cases where the accident was related to lifestyle problems, such as drugs and alcohol, rehabilitation is even more complicated. Therapy must be not only physical but mental as well. Here again, friends can be of much help by guiding the person into a healthier lifestyle.

Any persons with a disability are going to have to ask for help sometimes. They may have trouble accepting that fact, but once they do, they'll let others know when they need help. If they can't get a door open or pick up something from the floor, they'll politely ask. If they don't ask for help, there's no need to offer to, say, push a wheelchair, hold a book, or dial a phone. If you're not sure what you should be doing or offering, just ask! Reach a mutual understanding as soon as you can and get on with a normal friendship.

How can families help?

When a family member becomes paralyzed, it is a psychological shock to the whole family. The situation calls for new relationships and responsibilities as everyone works out a new family lifestyle. Very often, families can use professional counseling to understand their emotions, how they will have to relate to each other, and how they will have to work together as a family.

Can persons with spinal cord injury have sex?

Like any human being, they enjoy physical affection. To what extent they can have or enjoy sex or reproduce depends on the nature of the injury. Some can do it, some can't. This is probably none of your business. If it is, ask. If not, don't.

7

Will Thomas

Will Thomas lives on the better side of a medium-sized industrial city. He used to live on the worse side and is glad he got out of there before it was too late. In high school, he was a football player until he got into the wrong car with the wrong driver. He still has the big, heavy shoulders of a linebacker, yet he also has the soft-spoken voice of someone who isn't afraid to share his thoughts and feelings. He loves music—rap, R & B, and soul—and his bedroom walls are hung with posters of Mc Lite, Lords of the Underground, SWV, 2 PAC, and other hot musicians. He likes to have company, and his family had to have a special phone line installed because he gets so many calls. He's always got people coming over to visit, and when he doesn't, he just rolls down the ramp at the back door and goes out looking for friends.

"I flipped over in a Jeep. It was just two blocks from home. I was walking a friend of mine home. My mother and grandmother were on the porch when I left. I told them I'd be right back. We walked over to his house, and then I met another kid, and we were walking down the street and this other kid drove up in his Jeep and said he'd give us a ride home. We didn't know he was high. He took off real fast, but then passed out at the wheel. The car crashed into a double-parked car, and then another car. The Jeep flipped over and just kept flipping.

"I got trapped under the dashboard, and it took the fire department an hour and a half to cut me out. I was conscious the whole time, not really in pain except when I'd try to move my back. I couldn't feel my legs at all. The driver died of traumatic head injury, but the other kid got away with a dislocated shoulder. He's still walking.

"The ambulance took me to St. Vincent's Hospital. My spine was broken at the T-4 level, which means I couldn't move anything from my chest on down. If the injury was a little bit higher, I wouldn't be able to move my arms. I was in the hospital for four months, in a cast from my chest to my hips. I couldn't roll over in bed. I had to sleep on my stomach all night. In the morning, a nurse would come in and roll me onto my back so I wouldn't get bedsores.

"I was totally depressed and kept thinking about suicide. I didn't want to live if I couldn't walk. It's all I thought about. I didn't know how to deal with it. Meanwhile, my girlfriend couldn't handle it. She didn't have any way to come see me, and after a while we just broke up. I talked to a psychiatrist at the hospital and told him I just wanted to die, but he told me I didn't need to think that way. It wasn't so bad. I just had to deal with it. Besides, there was a possibility of me walking again.

"That girlfriend of mine ended up going with this other kid who I didn't know. But I met him when he got shot four times and ended up paralyzed, and she couldn't deal with that, either. She and her cousin came over to ask me about my accident and if it was going to be the same with him and about his spine and what they should do.

"She was real mad because her boyfriend was with his cousin when he got shot, and his cousin was involved with something that was happening in the street. She said it was his own fault for being where he shouldn't have been. I told her you can't blame him for getting shot. You can't hold that against him. I told her she's got to stick by him if she loves him.

"I went up to the hospital to see him. I told him how

she felt, and I told him he was going to get real depressed for a while, but that he shouldn't think his life was over. He could learn to get around, to dress himself, take a shower and everything. I told him how at first I thought I'd never play sports again, never have a girlfriend, never get a job, and never be independent. But none of that was true. I play basketball, I got a fine girlfriend, and everybody tells me it's actually easier to get some jobs if you're in a wheelchair, though I don't really know because I haven't tried yet. It could be the other way around. But I told my friend it's just like before except you do everything sitting down. He said he didn't like it, and I said I don't like it either, but that's the way it is. I told him about a guy I met after my accident. He's in a wheelchair, and he goes skiing on some kind of special sled with skis on the bottom. He goes swimming. He's not letting a wheelchair stop him from anything.

"The ones who think being in a wheelchair is different are the *other* people. They look at you different, like you're some other kind of person. They ask a lot of dumb questions. Some of my friends try to slip me money. I *hate* that. It just makes me feel odd. And they're kind of careful with me, you know? Some people are afraid to touch me because they think they might hurt me. They're always trying to help me. They want to push me around, but I hate that. If I can do something myself, I'll do it myself. If I need help, I'll ask for it. I took the armrests off the chair so people wouldn't have anything to push on.

"I can get around a lot by myself. I live with my mother and brother in my grandmother's house. They put a ramp up to the back door and widened a couple of doors downstairs so I can get around. I can get into the bathroom and take a shower by myself without any problem, and I can go outside and push around whenever I feel like it.

"My shoulders are even stronger than they used to be because of pushing around a lot. I go on down to the high school to meet friends. It's about three miles. I can get there in fifteen or twenty minutes. I go down the sidewalk, which I've gotten pretty good at. Without stopping I can lean the chair back and raise the front wheels up over a curb. Then I just give a hard push and the back wheels go up over it.

"My wheels are cambered, so they like tilt out at the bottom. That makes it easier to go fast, but you've got to know how to do it. The more cambered wheels are, the faster you can go but the harder it is to control. I tried out the chair of somebody who was like my manager, kind of, at the hospital. She used to be a police officer, but when she was chasing somebody down some stairs, she fell and broke her spine. The wheels on her chair are real cambered. I gave one push and went almost half the length of my street. But when I tried to turn, the chair whipped right around. I did a three-sixty and almost fell over.

"It takes about four months to become an expert in the wheelchair. I can balance on two wheels, tilt the chair back, and lean against the wall, stuff like that. People tell me it looks like fun, but I tell them they don't want to be like this.

"I got friends who like to joyride and speed around. I tell them, hey, that's not it. You drive like that, you're going to end up like this. Believe me, you don't want it. The other day, I was with this friend of mine who was speeding down the same street where I had my accident. I told him he better be careful or he could end up like me. He said he didn't care, he'd deal with it when it happened. I said that's easy to say now, but just wait till you're in my situation. You don't need to get into my situation to figure things out.

"I got in a fight once. There's this guy who just likes to make trouble for people. He used to always pick fights with me before the accident. So one day he saw me in my chair and he starts circling around me telling me he's got me now. He started hitting at me and saying he was going to flip me out of my chair. All of a sudden I grabbed him and pulled him down. I got real strong arms from pushing around all the time, so I took him down to the ground and held on to him and just kept hitting him, hitting him, hitting him. I wouldn't stop until somebody broke us up because I was afraid if he got up he'd be able to do whatever he wanted with me. Later on, he apologized. I told him, you better be careful. Whatever you do comes back to you in the worst way. You be messing with people in wheelchairs, someday it's going to be you in the wheelchair and people messing with you.

"I knew this one kid who used to mess with everybody. Then one day he got shot. He was paralyzed from the neck down. I went to see him in the hospital. I said, 'See? You messed with everybody and now you got what you asked for.' He got better later. His spine was only bruised. He's walking again. I told him he better know how lucky he was.

"I was never bad to anybody, so everybody just tries

to help me. They take me out, we go places. The phone never stops ringing. Some girls will call me and start crying and everything, but they won't come visit. They don't want to see me like this. I don't know why not. They just can't handle it. I don't know what they're thinking.

"I'm on a basketball team, the Park City Rollers. The rules are just about like regular basketball. You have to bounce the ball once, then hold it in your lap and push twice, then bounce it again. You still have to pass it and everything. The baskets are the same height. It doesn't matter if you're in a wheelchair. It's still competition, and you can still try to be better than the other guys. Even though it's a new team, we're real good. We went up to Boston and beat the Spokebenders, even though they've been in the league a lot longer than us. The score was something like forty to thirty.

"I've got to thank a whole lot of people who have been helping me through this. I couldn't do it without my mother and grandmother, my brother Ronald, my friend Shawn Holmes, and my nurses, Valerie Wilson and Jill Brown.

"I'm having a special walker brace made for me. With that I can start to learn to walk again. Once I have that,

I'm going back to school. I got one more year before I graduate. As soon as I graduate, I'm going to get a job so I can be independent. I'm going to get a car and a place to live, and I'm not going to have to depend on anybody. I'm going to walk again. I know it. I can do it."

Questions about Wheelchairs

How do people with disabilities feel about their wheelchairs?

Rather quickly, their chairs become an extension of their bodies. Some individuals are bothered—sometimes very much so—when others touch or mistreat their chair. To lean against it or rest your feet on some part of it, for example, would be seen as irritating rather than as a casual acceptance of the chair.

What's the best way to push or carry a wheelchair?

The basic rule: First ask if the person wants help, then ask how to do it.

There are electric wheelchairs and manual wheelchairs. Don't push an electric wheelchair. Since they're quite heavy, don't try to move one up or down stairs or over curbs. Nor should you ever try to operate one. Don't touch the control, even for a moment as a joke. The control is very sensitive and you could very quickly do damage to the chair and anything near the chair. You could also hurt someone.

In the case of a nonelectric chair, first ask if the person wants to be pushed. Very often they do not. But

90

they might need help over a curb or up a step. Sometimes a person transferring from a chair to a car forgets to lock the chair brakes and the chair rolls away. If you notice such a situation, do offer help. Don't try to move a wheelchair with a person in it up or down stairs unless you've been trained to do so. One mistake could have disastrous consequences.

Believe the wheelchair user when he or she warns you of the chair's capacity. If the user says you shouldn't try to go down a certain hill or up certain stairs, don't argue.

To cross sand at a beach, it's easier to pull the chair backward.

Be careful before lifting an empty wheelchair. If it has removable handles, they may come off in your hand. Ask the owner where to grab hold to lift. Some wheelchairs fold inward so they can fit in a trunk or on a car seat.

8

Debbie Eisenberg

Debbie Eisenberg, eighteen, was born with cerebral palsy. Except for that difference, she's quite like any other young adult. She likes soap operas, rock 'n' roll, computer games, the mall, matzo ball soup, and solitaire. In her room she's got a few bowling trophies, a homemade Grateful Dead poster, a class picture, a lot of stuffed animals. Her favorite movie: Philadelphia. Anybody who sits down and talks to her gets treated to a big, dimpled, hazel-eyed smile that most young girls would die for. And anybody who treats her like a freak might get a nasty little piece of her mind.

"You gotta understand: Our lives suck. I mean anybody with a disability. It's a constant battle. Everywhere you go, you hit an obstacle. Like I went to this conference down in Washington with a bunch of people from the Center for Independent Living, and we roll into the hotel and they haven't got any rooms on the ground floor. Okay, sure, so the upstairs rooms are accessible by the elevator, but suppose there's a fire? We're stuck there. And then they wouldn't let us use the phone in our rooms unless we had a credit card, which a lot of people with disabilities don't have because they don't have jobs. And then they towed away my van because it was parked illegally but where the hotel told us to park because they didn't have a handicapped spot.

"Everybody looks at me like I'm a freak. Either that or they don't look at me at all. The kids in school are idiots. They think I'm contagious. They don't even know what cerebral palsy is. They think it's like AIDS or something. I have no good friends my own age. Zero. I go to school, I come home, I go to doctors. That's my life.

"The biggest idiots of all are the teachers. They just make problems and don't make any effort to do what they're supposed to do. The school board takes the easy way out, and the teachers don't try to teach you anything. My mother has to get on the phone every five minutes and argue with them. For me to go on a field trip, I have to bring my own van and my own aide or a family member. My father told them that if I didn't go, nobody went. I'm lucky I've got a cousin and a good friend who are lawyers. I can call them anytime.

"I couldn't even go to the high school in my own town. They send all the wheelchair kids to the school in the next town over because they don't want to spend the money to make the school here accessible. But even that other school isn't completely accessible. There's only one bathroom we can use, and it's at the nurse's office. So half the time there's a line of us sitting in our chairs waiting for our turn. It takes a long time, plus I have to go a lot because I have to drink a lot of water to keep my kidneys functioning. It's an ongoing thing, but some of the teachers make me get a frigging pass every single time. And not only that, but they won't let me drink water during class even though the doctor says I have to.

"I've got a form of cerebral palsy (CP) called athatoid and spastic, which means my brain is always firing off signals for my muscles to move. They tighten up and most of the time move uncontrollably. I've never been able to take more than a couple of steps, and I can't do much with my hands. I can get food into my mouth, but somebody else has to cut it up. I can't get myself out of bed or take a bath by myself. But I'm better off than some people with CP. Some can't talk and can't move anything but their eyes. The only way some can communicate is by controlling a computer with their eye movements to spell out words letter by letter.

"I have to do constant physical and occupational therapy to keep my muscles from getting too tight or spastic. For physical therapy, they lift my legs up to loosen my hamstring muscles. For occupational therapy,

I have to practice dressing and eating. Periodically, every six months to two years depending on how high my muscle tone gets, I have to have an operation where they cut my muscles so I'm not so rigid.

"Besides the physical problems, I've got a learning disability, too. I'm not the slow learner a lot of people think I am, but I have trouble reading. Half the problem is the school. They don't teach you anything if you're in a wheelchair. The teachers wouldn't even learn how to work my laptop computer. They didn't care.

"And besides the problems related to CP, I've got problems from a back injury I suffered after falling down the stairs at the capitol building in Hartford, Connecticut. I was trying to find the ramp. I tried to turn my chair around to get out of the way of another wheelchair and ended up going headfirst down the stairs in my electric chair. I was knocked unconscious for a while. During that time, my grandfather, who wasn't alive, came to me and told me that it wasn't my time to go yet. Then I woke up, but I didn't know what was going on. I was just screaming for the governor. Now I have a pinched nerve in my neck and my whole body is messed up. Everything has to be realigned. I have problems with my eyes, my legs, my kidneys, my bladder, and other things. The doctors are still diagnosing me.

"I'm engaged to a guy I met at Camp Hemlock,

which is a special camp for kids with disabilities. He's nice, but he doesn't know what's out there in the real world. He's got CP, too. I'm really getting him on the ball, teaching him about the buses, about the tools we use for going to the bathroom, about how to get around. We told our parents what we were thinking when we went out for my birthday. They were all real happy. Everybody's happy but me.

"I can't be happy because I just don't know what's going to happen. For one thing, we can't get married for three years because my family wants us to wait and because I have to straighten out some legal things. I don't know where we're going to live or what we're going to do. It's hard to find a place that's accessible, and it's hard to go out anywhere. If you're in a chair, you can't go to a concert, can't go to a hotel, can't go to most people's houses, can't go to a lot of restaurants. If you go to the movies, you have to sit in the back row. You go to the mall and somebody's parked in the handicapped place. You try to go to the bathroom and it's too small. I can't even go to synagogue. There's no ramp. So I don't know what we're going to do.

"If you want to see what it's like to have a disability, try going around in a wheelchair for a day. See all the places you can't go. See how people talk to you. See how much fun it is. It isn't fun. There's an unbelievable number of things in your way no matter where you go.

"Whenever my family wants to go on a trip, it's a big pain. We have to take an aide, pack the chair, bring backups of my equipment, my special glasses, special pillows, catheter stuff, and special supplies. Last time we went somewhere, the airline just *dumped* my chair and broke it. They helped my parents buy a new one, but then when I had my accident, I broke it. You can't insure wheelchairs, so we're out $11,000.

"Drug stores love kids like me. Whenever I call up my pharmacist, he says, 'What do you want this time?' He goes over my long list of drugs. Usually I don't need a prescription unless the refills on the old one ran out or if a doctor changes the medicine.

"I was on Valium for ten years, but boy does it mess you up. I don't recommend using it. You get depressed, and it messes up your digestive system, and then everything else shuts down. I had to stop taking it.

"I'm still messed up inside. Nobody knows it except for me. I'm sad all the time. All the time. My family knows, but they don't know what to do about it. I go to a psychiatrist. He's okay, I guess, but I'm still sad all the time. Every day there's another problem. Can't go here, can't go there. Got to go to another doctor. More bull from the school. More bull from a doctor. Got to explain to another phone operator why I can't dial the number myself. If an aide doesn't show up, you're stuck in bed. My live-in aide mistakenly erased everything on all of our five computers, and then she stole our credit cards. Another one stole the five computers. It all just gets so depressing.

"Yep, five computers. My mother has one, my father has one, and I have three: one for school, one for games, one for backup. But you gotta understand, computers is all I have to do all day.

"I'd like to give the world some advice: Don't think every disability is a contagious disease. Don't stare and don't look away. Don't talk to the wheelchair instead of the person in it. Don't talk to us as if we were babies. Don't slam doors on us. Don't put us down. Don't help without asking first.

"I've got some advice for anybody with a disability, too: Make sure you have the right doctor. Don't get on a plane with an electric chair. Don't let anybody give you bull. Know your medications. Be careful with side effects. Find the right wheelchair company and get the chair that's right for you, not right for somebody else. Get a catheter that's right for you, not for your doctor. Fight your battles through legal channels so the next person doesn't have to do it. Make a fuss and then stick with it or they won't change anything. Get a portable ramp. Know your limitations, but when you want to do something, JUST DO IT!"

Questions about Cerebral Palsy

What is cerebral palsy?

Cerebral palsy, sometimes referred to as CP, is any muscle disorder caused by damage to the brain. It is a developmental disorder that affects how a child grows and learns. The initial brain damage often occurs during pregnancy or shortly after birth, most often as a result of lack of oxygen.

Is there a cure for cerebral palsy?

There is no cure for the damage to the brain, and brain cells do not regenerate to heal. Therapy, special equipment, and training can help the person with CP control muscles and communicate.

Does cerebral palsy affect the ability to think?

Cerebral palsy affects people in different ways. The same brain damage that causes muscular problems may also affect the ability to think. In many cases, however, the disability is only physical. It's impossible to evaluate mental ability by physical appearance or speaking ability.

What's the right way to talk to someone with cerebral palsy?

Talk just as you would to anyone else. Talk to the person, not to an aide or the wheelchair. Be patient if the person's speech is labored or hard to understand. If you can't understand, politely ask the person to repeat it. You can offer help if it seems needed, but don't do anything unless you're asked.

Federal Laws for People with Disabilities

On January 26, 1992, the Americans with Disabilities Act (ADA) went into effect. As of that date, discrimination against people with mental or physical disabilities was to cease. All public buildings, from government offices to museums to stores to stadiums, were to be accessible to all people. Companies were required to offer any affordable help to employees with disabilities, such as readers for the blind, interpreters for people with hearing impairments, special or modified equipment for those who need it, and so on.

The ADA is actually a civil rights law very similar to the civil rights acts of 1964 and 1968 that ensured equal rights to people of all races and religions. It took the United States almost two hundred years to formally recognize the importance of equal rights for all Americans . . . and thirty more years to recognize that people with disabilities are entitled to those same rights.

In the ADA, a broad interpretation of disability was adopted. "Disability" was defined as a physical or mental impairment that substantially limits one or more major life activities; a record of such an impairment; or being regarded as having such an impairment.

Physical impairments include physiological disorders, contagious diseases, cosmetic disfigurements, and anatomical loss in any of the body systems, such as neurological, musculoskeletal, respiratory, cardiovascular, and digestive.

Mental impairments comprise any mental or psychological disorder, including mental retardation, organic brain syndrome, and emotional or mental illness, and any learning disability even if caused by a traumatic environment such as a dysfunctional family.

It is interesting to note that substance abuse is considered both a physical and mental impairment.

Major life activities include self-care, manual tasks, walking, hearing, seeing, speaking, breathing, learning, and working.

When the ADA refers to "a record of impairment" and "being regarded as impaired," it is recognizing the fact that a person may be subjected to discrimination because of disabilities that have improved, are irrelevant to a particular job, or never even existed. In other words, if a person is considered to have a disability, by definition he or she *does* have one, and it is illegal to treat that person differently because of it.

Congress also passed two major laws guaranteeing the education of children and youth with disabilities. The Education for All Handicapped Children Act (EHA) of 1975 asserts that a "free appropriate education," including special education, is available to young people with disabilities, regardless of the severity of the disabilities. To the greatest extent possible, the education should take place in the regular education environment. The act also protects the rights of young people and parents, assures the effectiveness of special education, and financially assists state and local governments.

In 1990, Congress passed the Education of the Handicapped Act Amendments of 1990, which is now known as the Individuals with Disabilities Education Act (IDEA). It extends the rights and services established in the EHA of 1975.

All United States citizens and companies share responsibility for making ADA requirements a reality. People without disabilities are obliged to recognize their prejudices and make an effort to put them aside. Companies are obliged to do what is necessary to help people with disabilities come to work, do a job, and enjoy public facilities such as restaurants and stores. And people with disabilities are responsible for speaking up and helping the rest of the world recognize the handicaps they face and how they can be overcome.

This means more than ramps and special toilet stalls. It means making the extra effort to understand the person with speech problems, writing down something for a deaf person, or reading something for a blind person. It means offering a special job to someone of limited mental capacity. It means reaching out a little further for friendship.

No law can cover every eventuality in our society. In situations in which it seems that the Americans with Disabilities Act is being disregarded, the person responsible for changing the situation should be informed. If the problem is not corrected or a reasonable understanding reached, someone should contact the local government. There are also federal programs and organizations that deal with adherence to the ADA. These organizations are listed in the "Resources" section of this book.

Resources

Spina Bifida Association
of America
4590 MacArthur Blvd., #250
Washington, DC 20007-4226
(800) 621-3141
(202) 944-3285

Cystic Fibrosis Foundation
6931 Arlington Rd.
Bethesda, MD 20814
(800) 344-4823
(301) 951-4422

United Cerebral Palsy
Association
1522 K St. NW, Suite 1112
Washington, DC 20005-1202
(800) USA-5-UCP

National Retinitis Pigmentosa
Foundation
1401 Mt. Royal Ave., 4th Floor
Baltimore, MD 21217-4245
(800) 683-5555
(410) 225-9400
TDD: (800) 655-5551
(410) 225-9409

March of Dimes Birth Defects
Foundation
1275 Mamaroneck Ave.
White Plains, NY 10605
(914) 428-7100

American Council of the Blind
1155 15th St. NW, Suite 720
Washington, DC 20005
(202) 467-5081

American Foundation
for the Blind, Inc.
15 West 16th St.
New York, NY 10011
(212) 620-2000
(800) 232-5463

National Association
of the Deaf
814 Thayer Ave.
Silver Springs, MD 20910
(301) 587-1788
TDD (301) 587-1789

Disability Rights Education
and Defense Fund
(800) 468-4232

Apple Computers
Worldwide Disability Solutions
Group
(800) 776-2333

AT&T Computers
Products & Services
Special Needs Center #15
(800) 233-1222

National Committee for
Citizens in Education
(800) NETWORK

National Parent Network
on Disabilities
1600 Prince St., Suite 115
Alexandria, VA 22314
(703) 684-6763

National Center for
Youth with Disabilities
University of Minnesota
Box 721
420 Delaware St. SE
Minneapolis, MN 55455
(800) 333-6293
(612) 626-2825

Children's Hospice
International
700 Princess St.—Lower Level
Alexandria, VA 22314
(800) 24-CHILD

National Organization
on Disability
(800) 248-2253

Office of Minority Health
Resource Center
P.O. Box 37337
Washington, DC 20013-7337
(800) 444-6472

American Paralysis Spinal
Cord Injury Hotline
(800) 526-3456

TDD and TTY Operator
Services
Call this phone number by
TDD or TTY computer:
(800) 855-1155

Handicapped Media
(800) 321-8708

National Library Service for the
Blind and Physically
Handicapped
Library of Congress
1291 Taylor St. NW
Washington, DC 20542
(800) 424-8567

National Rehabilitation
Information Center
8455 Colesville Rd., Suite 935
Silver Spring, MD 20910
(800) 34-NARIC

AT&T National Special
Needs Center
5 Woodhollow Rd.
Room 1-I-19
Parsipany, NJ 07054
(800) 233-1222

National Tour Association
Handicapped Travel
Referral Service
546 E. Main St.
Lexington, KY 40508
(800) NTA-8886

Bibliography

Hundreds of books have been written on disabilities in general and specifically about the various syndromes, diseases, and other problems. A few titles are listed below. A librarian or bookstore salesperson can help you find other books. In your library card catalog, look under "disabilities" or under the name of a specific disability or a related topic, such as "deafness," "blindness," "wheelchairs," or "cystic fibrosis."

Bergman, Thomas. *On Our Own Terms: Children Living with Physical Disabilities.* Milwaukee: Gareth Stevens Children's Books, 1989.

Bernstein, Jane. *Loving Rachel: A Family's Journey from Grief.* New York: New American Library, 1988.

Deford, Frank. *The Life of a Child.* New York: Viking Press, 1983. (cystic fibrosis)

The Discover Book: A Helpful Guide for the World, Written by Children with Disabilities. Santa Rosa, Calif.: United Cerebral Palsy Association of the North Bay, 1989.

Exley, Helen (ed). *What It's Like To Be Me—Written and Illustrated by Disabled Children.* New York: Friendship Press, 1981.

Hale, Gloria. *The Source Book for the Disabled: An Illustrated Guide to Easier and More Independent Living for Physically Disabled People, Their Families, and Friends.* New York: Grosset & Dunlap, 1979.

Harr, Jaap. *The World of Ben Lighthart*. New York: Laurel-Leaf Library, 1979.

Kisor, Henry. *What's That Pig Outdoors: A Memoir of Deafness*. New York: Penguin Books, 1990.

Meyer, Donald J., Patricia F. Vadasy, and Rebecca F. Fewell. *Living with a Brother or Sister with Special Needs: A Book for Sibs*. Seattle: University of Washington Press, 1985.

Paulson, Gary. *The Monument*. New York: Delacorte Press, 1991.

Ratto, Linda Lee. *Coping with a Physically Challenged Brother or Sister*. New York: Rosen Publishing Group, 1992.

Roy, Ron. *Move Over: Wheelchairs Coming Through: Seven Young People in Wheelchairs Talk about Their Lives*. New York: Clarion Books, 1985.

Shenkman, John. *Living with Physical Handicap*. New York: Franklin Watts, 1990.

Shulman, Jeffrey. *It's Your Turn at Bat*. Fredericksburg, Md.: Twenty-first Century Books, 1988. (mobility impaired)

Stein, Sara Bennett. *About Handicaps: An Open Family Book for Parents and Children Together*. New York: Walker & Co., 1984.

Winthrop, Elizabeth. *Marathon Miranda*. New York: Holiday House, 1979.

Wright, Betty Ren. *Rosie and the Dance of the Dinosaurs*. New York: Holiday House, 1989.

Index